The Twelve Senses

The Twelve Senses

What it Means, Growing up a Human Being

David Donaldson

Wynstones Press

Published by
Wynstones Press
Stourbridge
England.

www.wynstonespress.com

First edition 2022

Cover illustration by David Newbatt.

Printed in UK.

ISBN 9780 946206 95 7

Contents

Acknowledgements

Many of these poems have sprung from the inspiring lectures of Albert Soesman recorded in his book The Twelve Senses (translated by Jakob Cornelis). He worked as a family doctor in the Hague until 1983 and gave workshops on the senses, developing Rudolf Steiner's research in this area.

Prefatory Note

This series of poems is conceived as one poem, an interwoven whole to be read in sequence so that the parts are read in context.

The Physical Senses

Embodied. In a mantle of skin,
Scaffolding of bones. Immersed

In life processes, warmth, hunger,
Thirst. Exploring what it means

To move, struggle upright and fall.
Stand balanced on two feet without

Holding on.

1. Touch

The sense of being embodied

Worm's one and only
World of sense. Tunnelling
In pitch darkness at one
With its boundless World

Of soil. But touched
By something Other?
That's the moment
Of Awakening! So too

For Snail, Sea Anemone
Withdrawing tentacles
Or retracting tiny horns.
Learn your boundaries! Touch

Teaches them. For us- there's
The rub, the grit of being
Embodied. As if we'd been
Cast out, suffered an exchange

Of boundlessness for this
Bodily limitation. Touching,
Being touched speaks to us
Of separation, urges

Self-protection, intimacy,
Reconnection– all at once.

2. The Life Sense

Constitutional Sense

Spread all over. Inseparable
From Touch. Baby knows
Well enough. Wakes and cries
Its hunger, thirst, discomfort.

Settles to sucking once
Reunited with the breast.
Then sleeps, so all's well
Afloat on the Milky Way,

A Spirit-Child not quite
Touched down and as yet
To discover all it means
Growing up, a human being.

*

The Life Sense: how we embrace
The joy of it; take for granted
The pristine silence of the body's
Healthy functioning! It's pain
That wakes us up, brings us

Down to Earth, teaches
Due care, balance, restraint.
How raw is pain whenever
It pitches in to body, mind
Or soul. It disconnects us from

Life's full flow, reconnects us
Through others' care. How else
Could we grow in empathy,
Embrace another's plight if
Not for the shared experience

Of pain? Would we choose
If we could, a pain-free life?
Pain *points to the dignity of Man,*
According to Novalis.

We should be proud of pain.

3. *Self-Movement*

The Muscle Sense

Baby's woken up. How many muscles
Must combine to advertise the fact!

Give a tickle and the noise subsides,
Muscles relax, a smile lights up

And spreads. Then all's waving arms,
Kicking legs, as if reaching for hand-

Or footholds in the air. Well-being
Tickled into motion. In due course,

Such movements acquire focussed
Purpose and Baby's up and out,

Tumbling from cot or rocking chair,
Aspiring Toddler, crawling, struggling

To stand, to balance, take the first
Precarious halting steps, filled with

Inspired intention: to be following on.
          To be as you.

*

Formed to be upright yet none born
More helpless. As children we follow on
Until branching paths lead away
From home. Ideals, deeper intentions

Bring us to pause, take time to step
Aside, go our own way, circumstances
Suddenly aligning with our inner
Disposition: intentions to be realised

Sounding on as of a piece with
The unconscious will that raised us,
Babes in arms, to stand
                    on our own two feet.

*

We talk of *finding our river* as well as
What's coming down the track, the one
Free in fluid motion, the other rigid,

Determined; destiny, *written in the stars*,
(A life's plan ideal for a shared good)
Intertwined with fate, the sufferings

We can't avoid, *sent to try us*, so we say?
Is it out of such our future life is formed?
Trials lived through, capacities won?

Does how we live our fate shape future
Destiny? All's in motion: Time's flow
Extending in an unbroken Round

From birth to death, death
to a new birth.....

4. *Balance*

Our first balancing act:
Standing.
                    Having made it
Up, up to the crowning
Summit of our vertical,

Swaying unsteadily
At the admiring applause
Before tumbling down
Once more
                        and trying again.

No fear of failure. No
Knowing, either,

How we're formed
To succeed
                       in the ear's
Construction, the arch
Of the foot spanning
Ball and heel,
                            just
The driving will to be
Where we need to be;

Like others, upright
On our own two feet.

*

It's our first act of mastery.
Look, no hands! Upright
We begin to *find our feet,*
Establish our *points of view.*

Balanced, we extend to fill
The spaces we're in, leaning
On all we see, near at hand,
Far and wide: the vistas

Opening to view! Not so
At a cliff edge, tower top,
Looking sheer down
Where balance vanishes

In a lurching whirl and every
Point of view disappears
Except for the need to
Step away, clutch hold

Against the gaping void
We cannot fill.

*

Precarious contingency.
Have we forgotten?

Tightrope walkers
On the high wire,
Clasp fingers about
Their stabilising pole

Setting one foot in front
Then the other, eyes fixed
In front, their point
Of view drawing them on

As far off in the dead-ahead
As the sheer drop below.
Unwavering concentration
Sees them through to our

Open-mouthed applause.

*

Balancing always requires
Reference to things external
To ourselves, from the chair
We let go of as aspiring toddlers

To the waves alarming Peter
As he stepped out of the boat.
Walking on water's a manner
Of speaking about complete

Self-mastery. No performance-
Enhancing drugs. No machines
To reset our sense of balance,
Rocket us into weightlessness

For a tourist's view of the Earth's
Fragility, possible only with
A *balance sheet* to provide the means.
Machines are helpful servants

But diabolical when our centre
Of gravity's been displaced
And we've transfered to them
Our grounded sense of balance.

So the turning World's giddy
And we, as if mesmerised
Look down from the sheer brink
Of the teetering topmost tower

On which we've come to live
Out of all just proportions,
Its foundations shaking, shifting
From all that our driven thirst

For mastery continues to induce.

*

Self-mastery. Spirit-Self beyond
Ego. Setting foot on the path, at least.
What other key to the Kingdom

Of what it means to stand upright,
Grounded in truth of our origins:
The paradox of Touch, separated out

Yet needing, reaching for trusting
Loving reconnection with the World?
What other key to the Kingdom?

Whatever might of fear the World's
Powers induce to maintain control,
Create the foretold soulless dystopia,

Upright, on our two feet, we're made
To be free, equal, and live fraternally!

The Soul Senses

The World comes to meet us,
Greet us, teach and tempt us.
Who can help, sometimes, but

Lose their upright, become entangled,
Or giddy, fall flat in the headlong
Rush to sample this and that?

Eyes look, like, and blunder in;
Warmth flares to passion to have
And hold. If nothing else, then

Pain with its myriad sharp reminders
Recalls us to our senses, meaning
Our foundational sense prepared

Over countless ages: the ineffable
Balance of the body's inner warmth.

1. Smell

Nostrils conduct no border checks
For smells. Whatever's streaming
On the breeze streams in unchecked.
Like honeysuckle of a summer's evening.
Momentarily, we're stunned. Pause

Our walking, talking to turn and look.
What? Where? There, alight on the hedge,
The golden candelabra we'd passed by
Unnoticed. But not the arresting smell.

It's short-lived, of course. Bury your nose
In a rose: there's brief seconds of inhaled
Enchantment leaving you lost for words.

*

What is it about Smell that's so arresting,
Yet so ephemeral? Its loss to us of its
Instinctual power? Many animals live
By smell. It's how Salmon reaches
Its spawning grounds. We've risen
To rely on our consciousness instead.

We still *smell a rat*; sense that something
Stinks. Instinctively, Smell sorts out good
From bad. Transformed to reasoning
This leads us on to soul concerns: rivers
Polluted, ravaged landscapes, toxic air.

Our Court of Consciousness in session
Tries to battle it out: propose Green
This and that, enact a Law of Ecocide,
Irradiate the Earth from space the better
To communicate..What is it that rules,

When, *led by the nose* in pursuit of some
Attractive gain, we're stunned by the trail
Of fragrance, to just what's going on. Do

You *smell a rat*? Or where, a whiff of rose?

*

Our Nose

No animal has one: snout, muzzle,
Trunk, beak..all for feeding with,
For attack or self-defence. But noses

Are not weaponised and cannot eat
Or drink; they're central to our features,
Point forwards, beyond ourselves.

How unimaginable, how disfigured
A human face without a nose! Flat,
Directionless. To *poke our noses* into

Others' business is the shadow they
May cast. But chin up and moving on,
They're pointing all the way from

Instinct to intuition. As we say:
Follow your nose.

2. *Taste*

Our choice? At least as far as
Opening our mouths. But who

Can resist the Fall that Taste
Represents? Mmmm....

Says it all. *Naughty but nice*
Laughs it off. And now,

We're scanning the packaging.
Wholesome or not? Feet

On the long trek back to the lost
Instinct for what's healthy and

What's not. Denatured foods
Are brother to Big Pharma:

The latter calls the other out
But both are invested in the profits

That go to fuel a toxic way of life.

*

Caterpillars do not taste.

They munch their whole way through
Without another thought.

Thinking's not what they do.

While Butterflies have known
The dark sleep of the chrysalis;

They were once Caterpillars too,
But munching's been outgrown

Now wings have set them free
To live by taste alone.

So the gold-green Earth
They munched to shreds

Turns to blossoms and fruit instead.

⋆

Caterfly? Butterpillar?

The one creature but the names
Won't mix. Form, life-styles

Radically diverge. What emerges
Drying its wings in the sun

Is a new creation.

*

There are profits and prophets.

The Psalmist cries

O taste and see
That the Lord is good...

There are countless Tastes
For savouring but where

Goodness begins
The munching stops.

3. *Sight*

Uncovers the miracle of What Is.
All dynamic motion in the embryo,
Living mobility in the bulb of the brain

As it pushes outwards two bud-like
Bumps forming the cupped structures
That will become our eyes. Brain,

So far surpassed the flowering plant
Yet still resonating with a shared
Impulse. Eyes are blossoms closed

At night. Opened to the light by day.

*

As day dawns..*let there be LIGHT*

And rainbows, too spanning the blue
Born of the darkness of space...

Let there be gold, yellows, fiery reds
Shining through the atmosphere

And at our feet, the friable soil
Birthing COLOUR as flowering plants

Drink in the light. But most of all,
As rising light dissolves the night

And we awake to break of day...
Let there be SIGHT!

*

Life is colour. Death drains to grey;
The tones of the rainbow, life's

Sustaining harmony, re-emerges
Endlessly from within itself.

The colour-circle's Nature's
Alphabet and wordless language

Intrinsic to our mirrored moods
Of soul in what eyes tell

Of states ever-shifting between
Sun, rain-cloud and storm.

*

Colours ray out in Spring
Then merge back into
The life-flow of restful green.
Or while Red stops us
In our tracks, Green,
Its complement, signals Go.

Blue's the hoped-for sky
Beneath which to light
The orange flames
Of the barbecue and cooling
Shades of lilac compose
The shadow in which
To shelter from the Sun.

Life and colour: inseparable.
Each intrinsic to the other
As light and dark. Eyes
Arise out of this mystery:

Gaze intently at a red surface
Then shift to plain white:
A green after-image arises,
(Or orange for blue,
Lilac for yellow): eyes,
Embedded in the colour circle

Following colour harmonies,
Complementary laws,
Active and passive inter-
Woven below the threshold
Of conscious sight. Harmony
Upheld by Laws, transgressed
In thinking freedom means
Endless choice to live as we insist.

4. *Warmth*

The Temperature Sense

Our primal sense. And foundation
For every other. Sets everything
In motion: the inner Sun to our
Planetary organs and Star-being
Called down to birth and a life

Lived within its orbit. Mothering
Warmth! Distributed within us
With such balance and precision
It's our unfailing measure for meeting
Needs just as pressing as hunger

Or thirst; necessities we have to earn
To sustain its balance of living warmth:
The clothes we need. A place to live.
Until, whatever outer conditions present
Of heat or cold, we feel 'just right'.

*

Young steers bunched together
Jostle for a better view as you
Place a hesitant foot on the stile
And wonder about your safe

Passage through. Warmth's
Their soul-condition radiating
Interest, curiosity or boundless
Joy for the dog, ears flapping

Spray flying as it chases a stick
Into the sea. Warmth can do
No other than seek out
Connection with the World.

For Adam Smith it's expressed
In giving and receiving, the gold
Of fair exchange; our innate need
To *love and be lovely*. What's worse

Than being *left out in the cold?*

*

Fire and Ice.

Feverish Passion,
Cold calculating Thought

And in between

Kindling Warmth
To interweave and

Humanise the extremes.

The Spiritual Senses

Senses of the Mind

How do sound waves translate
In our hearing, into song or speech?
How have we transcended instinct
In language, meaning; how come
To our consciousness of self?

What is Mind? Whence our world
Imaginations in myth and poetry;
In number, faith and reason?
And how can the World be thought
Or known through the mastery

And marshalling of data, through
The reasoning of reason alone
And not through the evolving Self
In the fullness of Imagination?
However we grow in mastery,

Power, control, have we still
The sense of Self to know that,
Lacking Love, what disasters ensue
When the wise serpent of knowing
Has lost touch with the peaceful dove?

1. Hearing

We hear with the part we used to eat with.
(A lecturing Professor's favourite joke)

Eyes push out from the surface,
Ears the reverse. Their tiny
Ossicles, body's smallest bones,

Were fashioned from the jaw
However so long ago.
So when you bite an apple

And hear *crush, crunch*, having
Set anvil, hammer and stirrup
Astir for all they're worth,

What's happening is Jaw's Tale
Repeating as you're eating.
But there's more (of course),

For Ears dive deeper from
Middle ear to inner; vibrations
Pass through fluid in the spiral

Cochlea whose multitude
Of hairs feel out the frequencies
And pass their coded messages

Upstairs for Brain's reflection.
The next we know it's *crush, crunch*,
The Jaw's Tale still repeating

Until we've finished eating.

⋆

Hearing takes in more than noise.
As if we're like some rock-bound ore
Released, refined, tempered to such

A pitch we're finally raised upright,
Able to hear the purest ringing tones
Or peal of bells that also have been

Freed, cast in the foundry, raised
Sky-high to ring out over the land
From the belfry tower.The mysteries

Of the inner ear place side by side
The balance of our upright stance
With the spiral threshold of

The Cochlea, as though two feet
Once firmly planted on the ground
Were all of a piece with being

Ready and able to be transported
On wings of song far beyond all that
Noisy, jaw-bound *crush and crunch.*

*

Sounds don't deceive like sight.
They're not surface-thin
Like ice sheets over

Sheer drops, or green
Lawns of sphagnum moss:
One false step and what

Rings true are your cries
    For help.

*

Sounds sound out the heart
Of things, from dull clanks
To crystal ringing tones
Carrying on the breeze.

Sprinkle fine sand over
A thin steel plate and draw
A bow (violin or cello)
Down its edge to sound a note.

Unpracticed, your scraping's
Mere noise. It produces
No effect until, suddenly,
It transmutes into pure

Tone and there, in place
Of random sprinklings,
A balanced form of ordered
Beauty stares you in the face.

*

Sight opens onto a visible World
Seeing which, we set out to explore,
Expand our understanding.

Hearing does the same but in reverse:
Draws us ever deeper into listening,
Into attentive stillness contracting

To a zero point, stillness beyond
Stillness; point of seed awaiting
The Word that will summon it

Into renewed being once more.

2. Speech

The language sense

Meaning. Born in Paradise
Before the bough broke

And we awoke to a World
Down and out in which

We had to find our way
As the primal Dream,

Cradled in the lap of the gods,
Became veiled in Myth

And the rational light of day.

*

Words arrive, born from far
Ocean reaches on a fast
Incoming tide, a vessel

We learn to climb aboard,
To steer, with which we chart
Our course. Words, still

Glinting with half-remembered
Paradise as if still in reach
Of *Bab-ilim*, the very gate

Of God. But no, we're swept
As on a Flood from the One
Into the Many, from Bab-ilim

To Babel, its multiplicity
Of tongues, cultures, enmities
Locked in states of mutual

Suspicion, hostility, war;
Even while the given glint
Of primal Meaning speaks

In each of us its universal
Language of loving
                and being loved.

*

In the beginning was the Word...

That solemn utterance
Like an Old Master caked
In layers of darkened varnish!

Stripped back, it's a summing up,
A simple statement of our
Reality. It's meaning, melodies

We hear. Not vibrations drumming
In the ear. Not single tones, or stray
Vowels and consonants. They're

Subsumed, as if erased so the song
May be heard rising, falling between
The intervals, or the words, like that

Scattered sand, jump into form
And focus from the sounds combined,
Or the story emerge out of the ordered

Stream of words. *Those who have ears*
To hear, let them hear, that hearing
Transmute into listening, listening

Into the creative silence out of which
Both words and music well: silence
Endless as it is unfathomable; that

Zero point from which the Word
Speaks into our reality of words
And music, into our reasoning

Light of life.

3. *Thought*

The concept sense

What Thought can think is polar
Opposite to the sense of life.
For whatever shape of triangle
Presents itself to sight, the number
Of degrees resulting, when

We add together the sum
Of its three angles will always
Be the same no matter what
Our feelings on the day or our
State of health. Facts are facts.

But where do they reside?
Beyond the forms we draw,
The words of explanation;
Beyond minds divided between
Subject, object..Beyond all these,

They reach into the Silence
Of What Is; the illimitable
Realm from which the World's
Made manifest; the wellspring
Pure Thought has drawn upon

As mind to Mind all thinking
Stilled in unwavering contemplation;
A coming home, *by the grace
Of Thought* which transmutes
Intuition into thinking's inspired

Activity, expressive of hitherto
Unthought ideas, imaginations,
Philosophies, breakthroughs
In science; poetry. A World
In Its becoming, brimming

With the concepts we inhabit,
Each formed and sounding,
Pictorial or abstract, after
The genius of our own
  Mother tongue.

*

Concepts may be open-ended
Or closed. Inhaling fresh air
As of a warming breeze
From the future, or stale air
From the past; they may hold

Fast with still-living roots
Capable of continued growth
Or be dried out, withering
Into the unchanging letter
Of the law, a status-quo

Of settled knowledge, belief,
Custom you challenge
At risk of ridicule or worse.
Concepts may expand our
Whole being. Help us grow

In self-control, inner freedom
Outer expressions of love,
Or close off the future in their
Own image, using all manner
Of inventions to determine

Who and what we shall become.

*

Language, said Emerson, *is fossil poetry*.
Submerged in data, how to surface?

Rise and sing and praise again
The unity of Being, of all beings?

It's by Imagination the World is known.
The rational light of day alone leaves us

Fragmented, lookers-on in a World
In service to the advance of its machines,

Following on in ever-quickening footsteps
And *whither bound?* Deeper into disconnection,

illusion
dependency?

*

Only by Imagination
Can the World be known;
Never by the wonders
Of the rational mind alone.

4. *Ego*

The sense of another's self

Core mystery. Always present,
Staring us in the face, invisible
And key to whatever of heaven
Or hell unfolds on Earth. Those
Welcoming arms our safe landing

Once the cord's cut, and our first
Grounding experience of being
Touched, held, wrapped in warmth
Of what it means to be loved.
It speaks the language of the Word

Before ever we can speak or think
Or whatever cruel displacements
Of poverty, ignorance, abuse,
Neglect, take hold to shroud
The radiance of the Spirit's growth.

*

In the beginning was the Word.
In our beginnings: Touch.
From within the loving arms,
The World is good, beautiful,
To be trusted: and confirmed

As we learn to run about, splash
In puddles, shuffle through leaves,
Delve in mud, build snowmen,
Learn to swim, climb trees
Higher and higher till we alarm

Ourselves and those below, perform
Feats of dexterity, shifting weight
And balance branch by branch,
Daring the swaying top, the vacant
Drop on jumping down; getting

Used to the feel of things, their
Intrinsic worth and reality:
Creeping things, earth and muck,
Stout sticks, the way through
The woods, ponds, tadpoles, frogs...

Coming to our senses in Earth's
Dimensions, so that what's
Emerging, grounded, growing,
Resounds to the core mystery
Of who we are in our being

And becoming.

*

Touch: *the sense of being embodied.*
Anchor, and polar opposite
To the sense of self which only
Lives and grows away from home.

So the senses come full circle,
Interweaving, interwoven as Child
Transforms to Woman, Man,
Flies the nest to meet the World

Grown up and growing: self to self.

*

Our other half! The paradox
Our sense of touch lays bare
From the moment of our birth:
Needing to reach across the great
Divide, body to body. And is it

The other in themselves we seek,
Or to bask in our reflection there?
But the mutual bliss once in retreat
Leaves us stranded for the loss of it.
Was it all self-love? Never left home?

Or in the wake of Love's mystery,
Had we made way for the other's
Self to be imprinted on our soul
And not as aching need, but vision,
Imagination made real, stepped

Down to Earth?

*

Language, thought: the branches, leaves.
But the blossom? The sense for others'
Selves, meaning: what it means to love?

And always to hold sacred the divine seed
Whether slumbering on in dead knowledge,
Or awakening to what's living in heart

And head combined: knowledge inwardly
Alive, reclaiming who we are, active
In striking sparks that will ignite

Imagination to flame and light our ways
Into paths where peace weaves conflict
Into harmony; and humanity, a single Sun,

Is rising to eclipse its own warring chaos
Of bewildering corruption. Such a future?
At once so far off and near; already here

Now, seeded in waking hearts and minds.

Notes

Page 27 O Taste and See... Psalm 34

Page 34 To love and be lovely... Adam Smith: see for example: *Adam Smith, What He Taught and Why it Matters* by Jesse Norman, p269 (Allen Lane 2018)

Page 44 In the beginning was the Word, the opening words of St. John's Gospel

Page 46 by the grace of thought: Owen Barfield quoting from Steiner's *The Philosophy of Spiritual Activity* in *Poetic Diction*, p209 (Barfield Press 4th edition 2010). The full quote: I ought never to say that I, as individual subject, think but rather that I, as subject, exist myself by the grace of thought.

Page 48 only by imagination (therefore) can the world be known: Barfield, as above p19

By the same author published by Wynstones Press

Poems for Younger Children

During his years of teaching within the Hereford Steiner Academy, David Donaldson composed a wide variety of verses for the children of his class.

Most of the enclosed poems were originally written for particular children, but we hope this book will allow these verses to bring joy and inspiration to many more children and adults alike.

46 pages.
ISBN 9780 946206 650

More Poems for Younger Children

This second volume by David Donaldson, originally published as *Promises*, contains a further varied collection of poems, composed during his years of teaching within the Steiner Academy Hereford. All of these verses were originally written for particular children, with inspiration from the wonderfully diverse subjects which the Steiner-Waldorf curriculum contains. We hope this book will help to bring joy to many more children and adults alike.

64 pages.
ISBN 9780 946206 971

A Treasury of Trees

Trees express the life of the Earth in all its variety, fruitfulness and mystery, from ancient beginnings to our present time. These 56 poems reflect the author's life-long love of trees; they are verses of celebration, remembrance and questioning reflection, drawing on first-hand observation and experience as well as historical research and well-known folk traditions and mythology.

A Treasury of Trees is a rich and imaginative exploration of our relationship to the Earth and all we stand to gain by entering more deeply into its life.

> "*This tree hymnal is indeed a work of devotion in which David Donaldson sings, it seems, almost every tree in Christendom, but often doing so, too, with a pagan magic.*"
>
> Matthew Barton, New View, Autumn 2018

78 pages.
ISBN 9780 946206 810

A Treasury of Plants

This rich Collection of over sixty poems explores the world of plants from a variety of perspectives, taking in the Earth's different climactic regions and the evolution of the plant world over time, delighting in its abundance and vitality.

It includes many common plants which have come to be woven into our own folk lore and mythologies and also explores how our own human processes of growth and development as free, conscious beings, are rooted in and belong to the same unfolding evolutionary process.

> *"We should live life on earth the way plants do. They remain fixed to the earth, but they transform it and evolve it."*
>
> Omraam Mikael Aivanhov

> *"There are many riches here, and the poems work best where they take imaginative flight, as they often do, in a flourish and ferment in which facts, images and sounds coalesce convincingly, creating the same kind of living union in words that plants themselves create, each in their own unique unfolding and uplift."*
>
> Matthew Barton, New View, Winter 2020/21

110 pages.
ISBN 9780 946206 889

Wynstones Press
publishes and distributes a range of
Books, Advent Calendars, Cards and Prints.
For further information please see:

www.wynstonespress.com
info@wynstonespress.com